This book belongs to:

Food Explorer:

Write your name above

Experience Delicious LLC

All Rights Reserved. This book or any portion thereof may not be reproduced or used in any manner whatsoever without the express written permission of the publisher except for the use of brief quotations in a book review.

Copyright 2021 Experience Delicious, LLC.
ISBN: 9781947001114
Visit us on the web! www.kidfoodexplorers.com

Dedicated to:

All the Kid Food Explorers learning their alphabet. Welcome to the wonderful world of reading!

...

My three girls, I can't wait to hear you read!

Hi Parents!

Help your emergent reader feel more confident, improve letter recognition, and enhance their learning experience as you read this ABC book together.

Here are a few ways to enhance your kids experience with this book. Have them:

Point to the letter with their finger
What letter is this?

Trace the letter with their finger
Can you trace "(say letter)" with your finger?

Identify lowercase and uppercase letters
Can you point to the uppercase letter?
Can you point to the lowercase letter?

Count the letters
Can you count the number of "(say letter)" on the page?

Identify the phonetic sounds each letter makes
This letter sounds like this "(say letter)" or this letter makes this sound "(say letter)."

Repeat letters and sounds
Say the letter and the sound. "S" makes the sound "ess." Now your turn.

Recall letters and sounds
Can you tell me what letter this is? Do you remember the sound this letter makes?

"Read" the story based on the images they see with a focus on the letter
What is the character doing that makes the same sound as the letter?

Remember to keep it playful and fun!
You can also grab our printable activity worksheets that accompany this book at www.kidfoodexplorers.com

Aa

A IS FOR APPLE
Av**a a**sks for **a**pple pie **a**t the **a**musement p**a**rk.

Bb

B IS FOR BLUEBERRY
Ben brings blueberries to baseball practice.

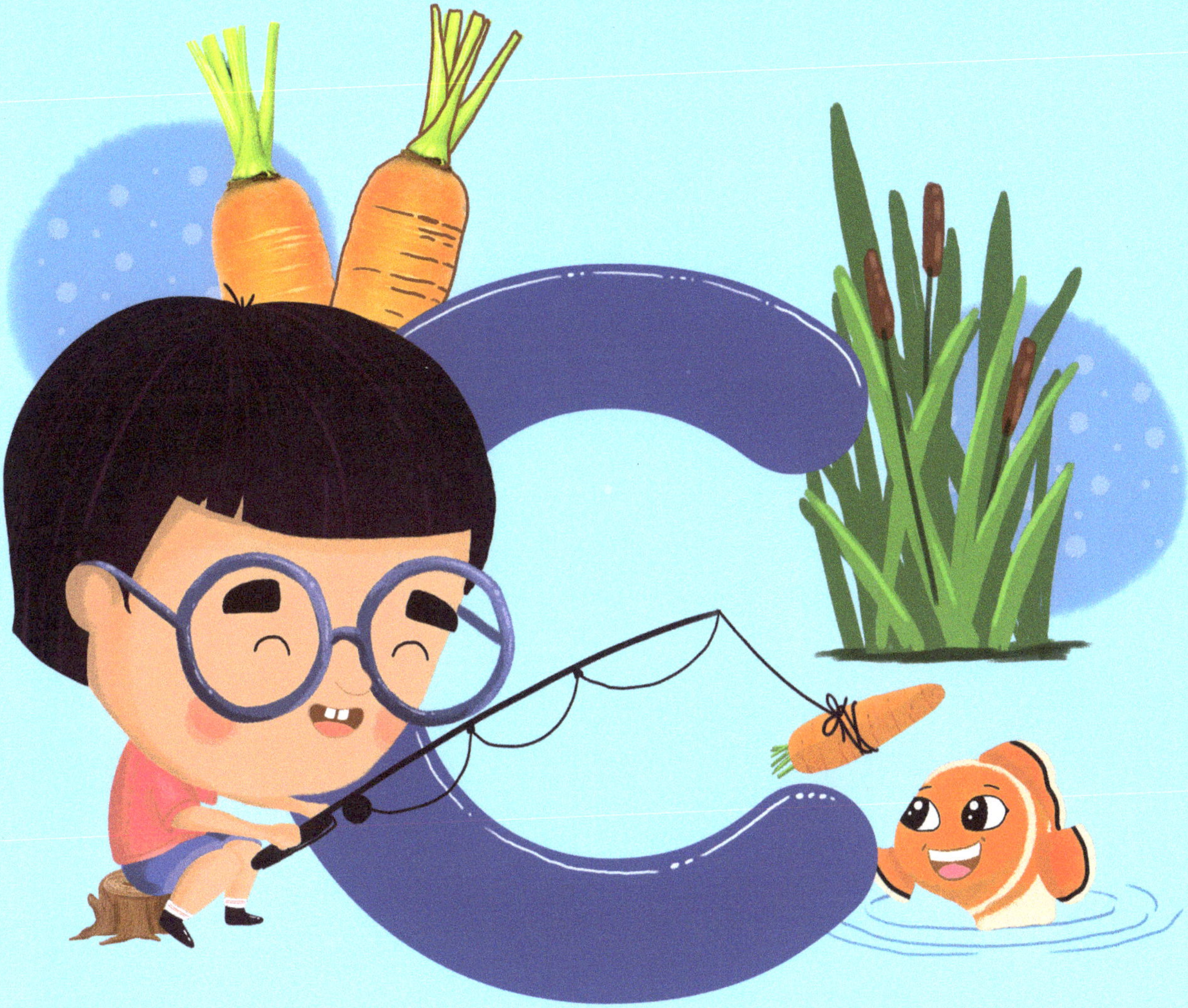

Cc

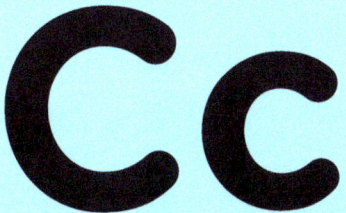

C IS FOR CARROT

Cho **c**at**c**hes **c**lownfish
with **c**arrots.

Dd

D IS FOR DAIKON
Daniel an**d** his **d**inosaur **d**ig for **d**aikon for **d**inner.

Ee

E IS FOR EGGPLANT
Eva **en**t**e**rtains **ele**phants with **e**ggplant.

Ff

F IS FOR FIG
Fiona **f**etches **f**igs with her **f**airy **f**riend.

Gg

G IS FOR GRAPES
Gabriel **g**athers **g**rapes from his **g**randmother's **g**arden.

Hh

H IS FOR HONEYDEW
Hanna **h**olds **h**andfuls of **h**oneydew for **h**orses.

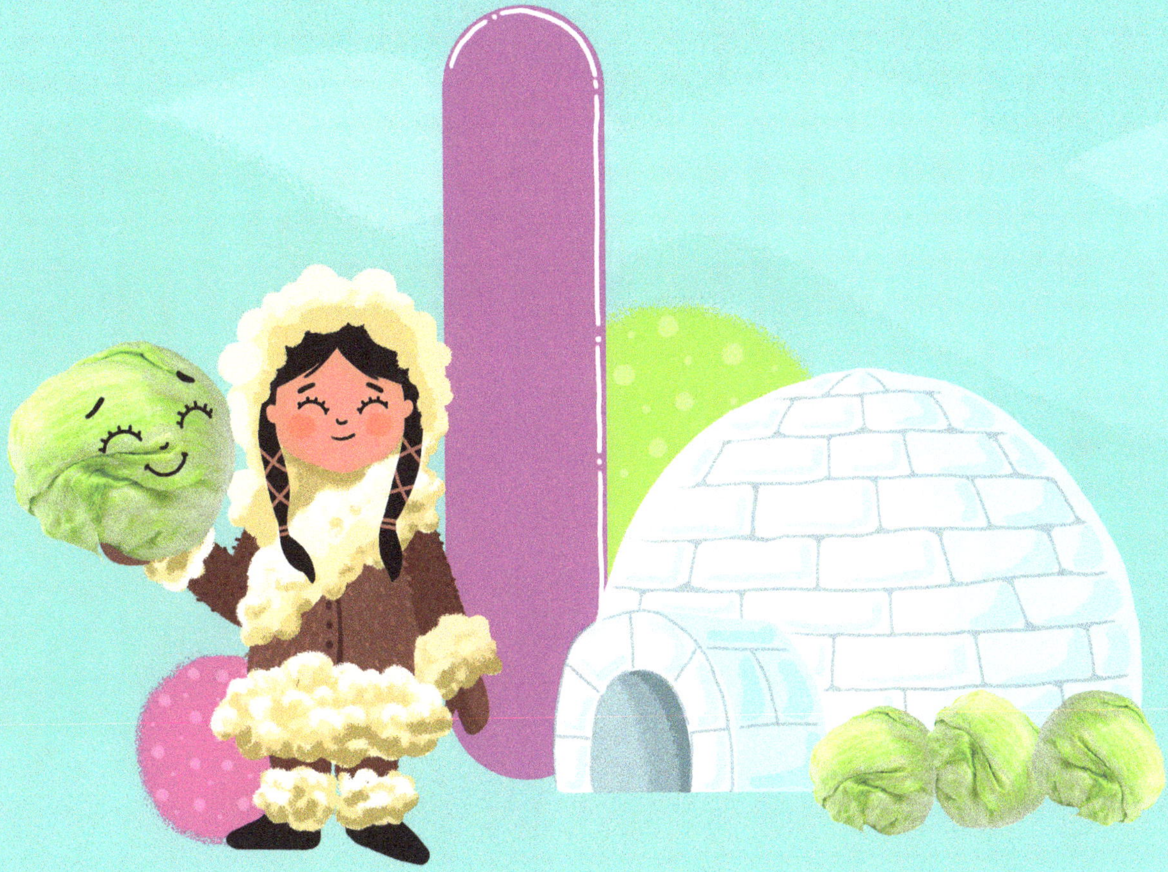

Ii

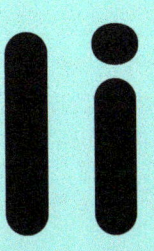

I IS FOR ICEBERG LETTUCE

Irene **i**nsulates her **i**gloo
w**i**th **i**ceberg lettuce.

Jj

J IS FOR JACKFRUIT
José jumps for jackfruit in the jungle.

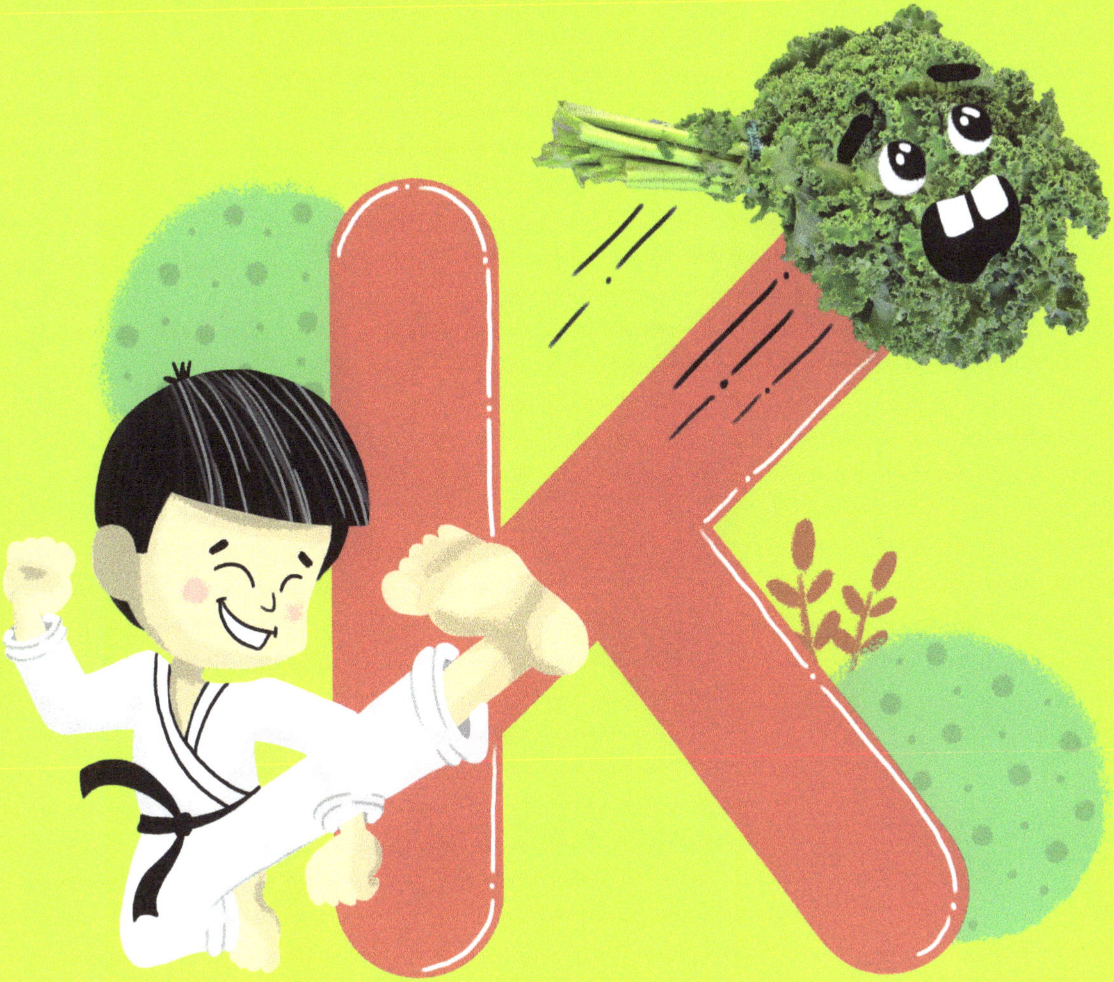

Kk

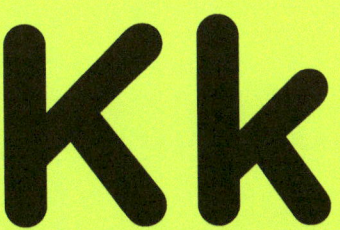

K IS FOR KALE

Kei **k**arate **k**ic**k**s **k**ale.

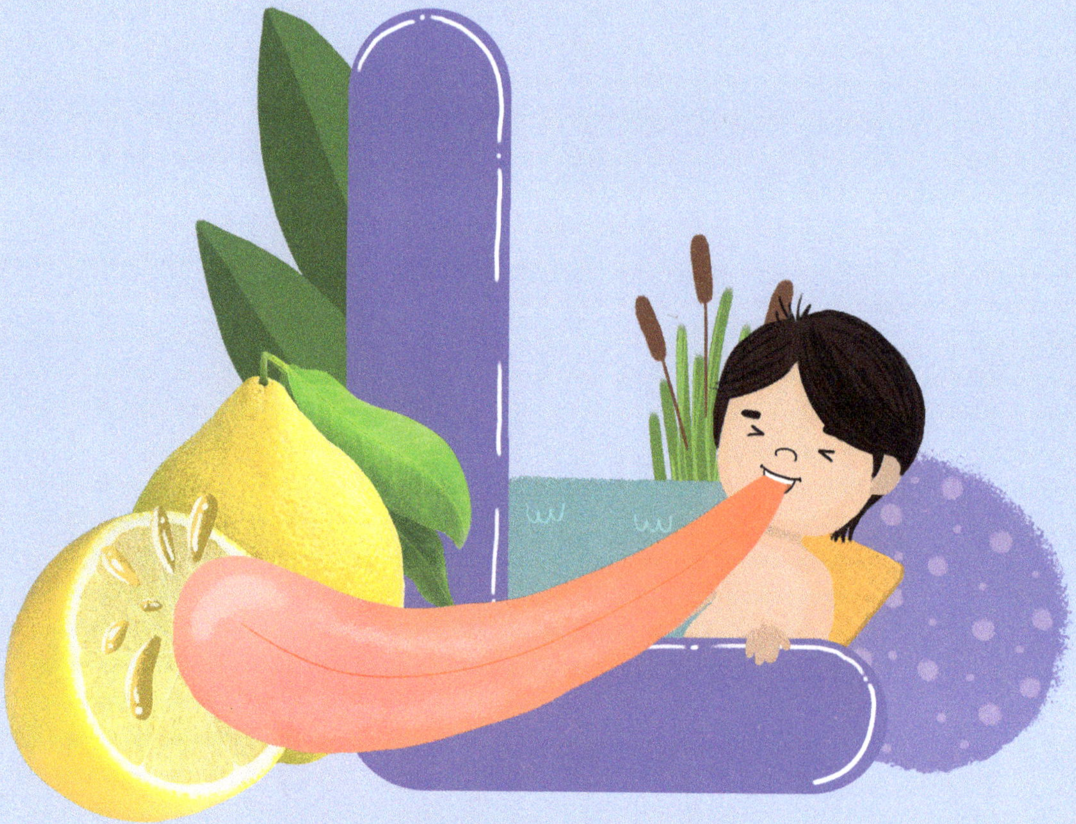

Ll

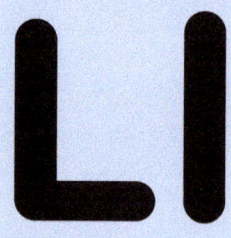

L IS FOR LEMON

Linus **l**icks **l**emons **l**ounging **l**akeside.

Mm

M IS FOR MANGO
Madalyn **m**akes **m**ango paintings at the **m**useu**m**.

Nn

N IS FOR NECTARINES
Noah **n**ibbles **n**ectari**n**es **n**ear a **n**arwhal.

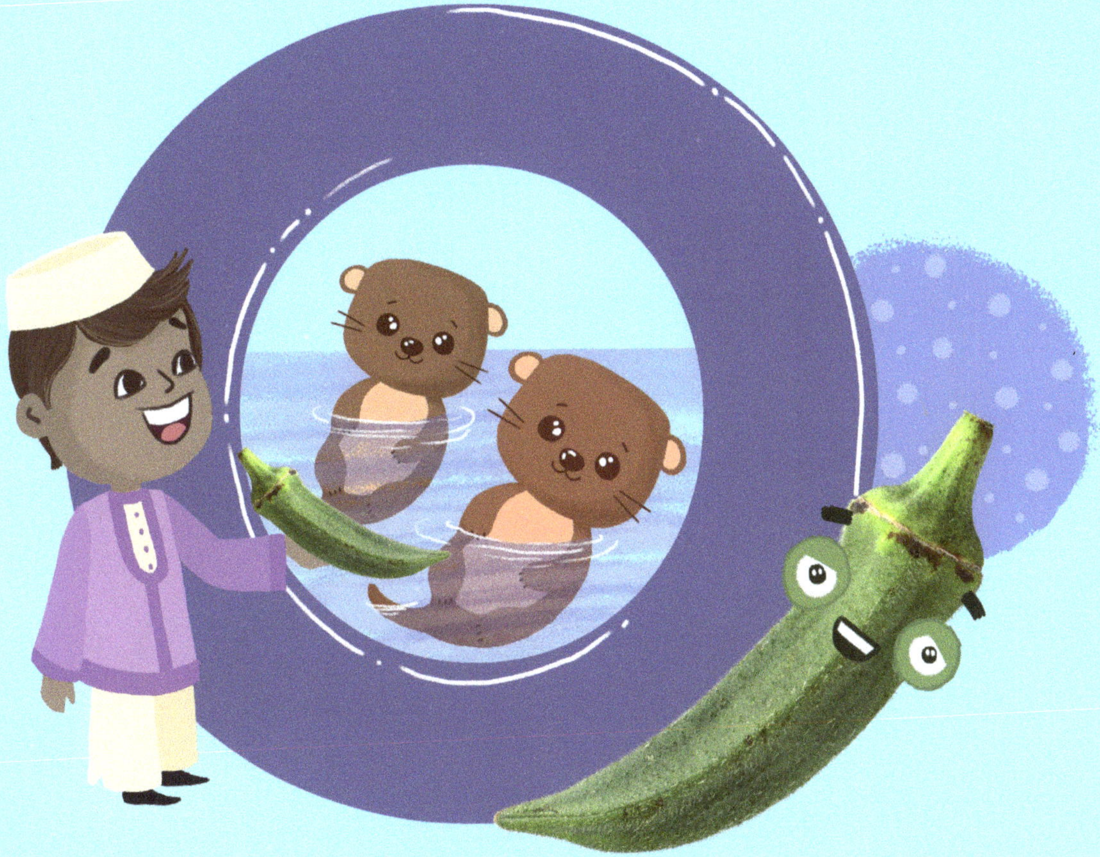

Oo

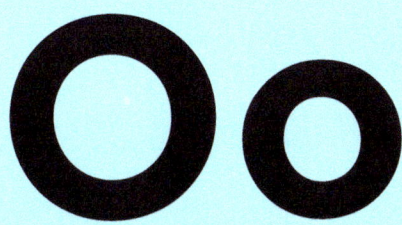

O IS FOR OKRA

Obi **o**ffers **o**kra t**o** **o**tters in the **o**cean.

Pp

P IS FOR PEPPERS
Priya **p**lays with **pepp**ers at the **p**layground.

Qq

Q IS FOR QUINCE
Quinton **q**uilts a **q**uince **q**uilt for the **q**ueen.

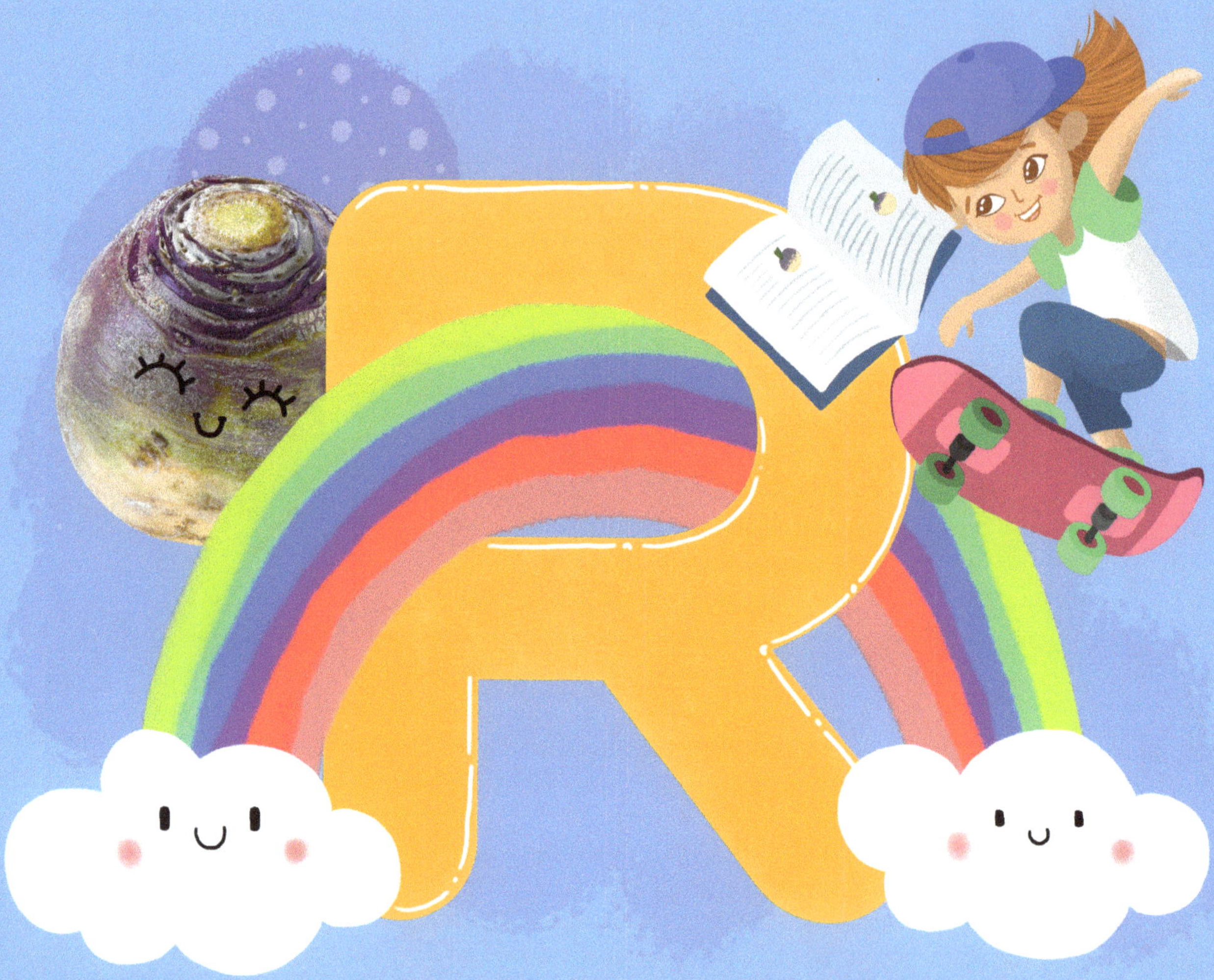

Rr

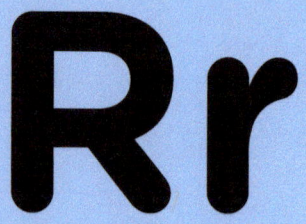

R IS FOR RUTABAGA

Raina **r**eads about **r**utabaga while **r**iding a **r**ainbow.

Ss

S IS FOR STRAWBERRY
Santiago **s**ave**s s**trawberrie**s** for a **s**nack after **s**kating.

T t

T IS FOR TOMATILLO
Tomás **t**akes **t**oma**t**illos on a **t**our of **t**he **t**own.

Uu

U IS FOR UGLI FRUIT

Uma **u**nwraps an **u**gli fru**i**t **u**nder an **u**mbrella.

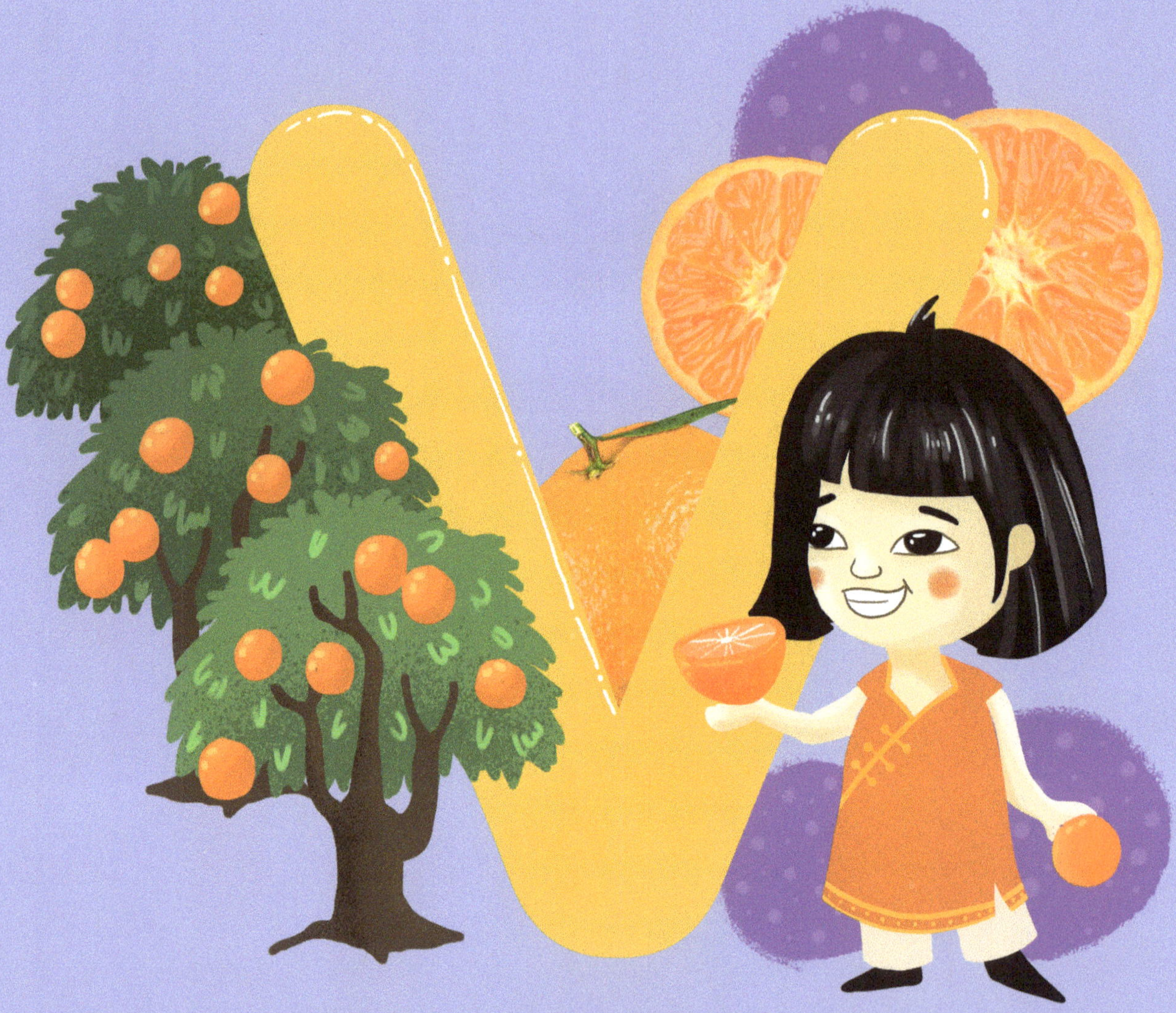

Vv

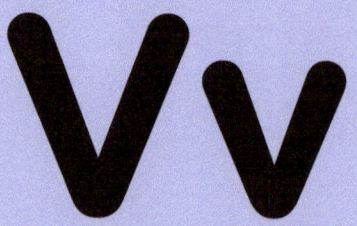

V IS FOR VALENCIA ORANGE

Victoria **v**isits a **V**alencia orange farm on **v**acation.

Ww

W IS FOR WAKAME
Wei **w**atches the **w**aves **w**hile eating **w**akame.

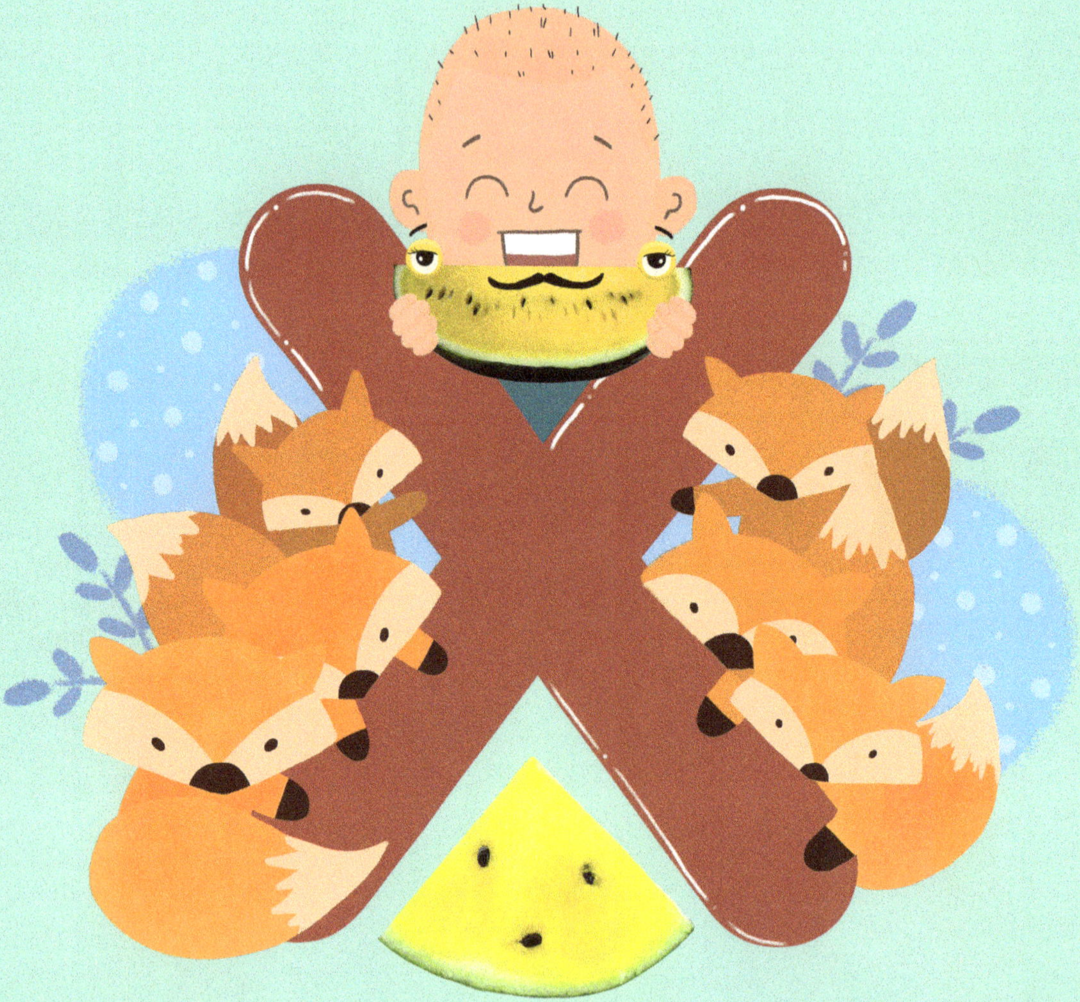

Xx

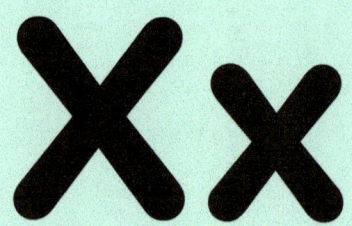

X IS FOR XIGUA

Xavier e**x**plores **x**igua with si**x** e**x**cited fo**x**es.

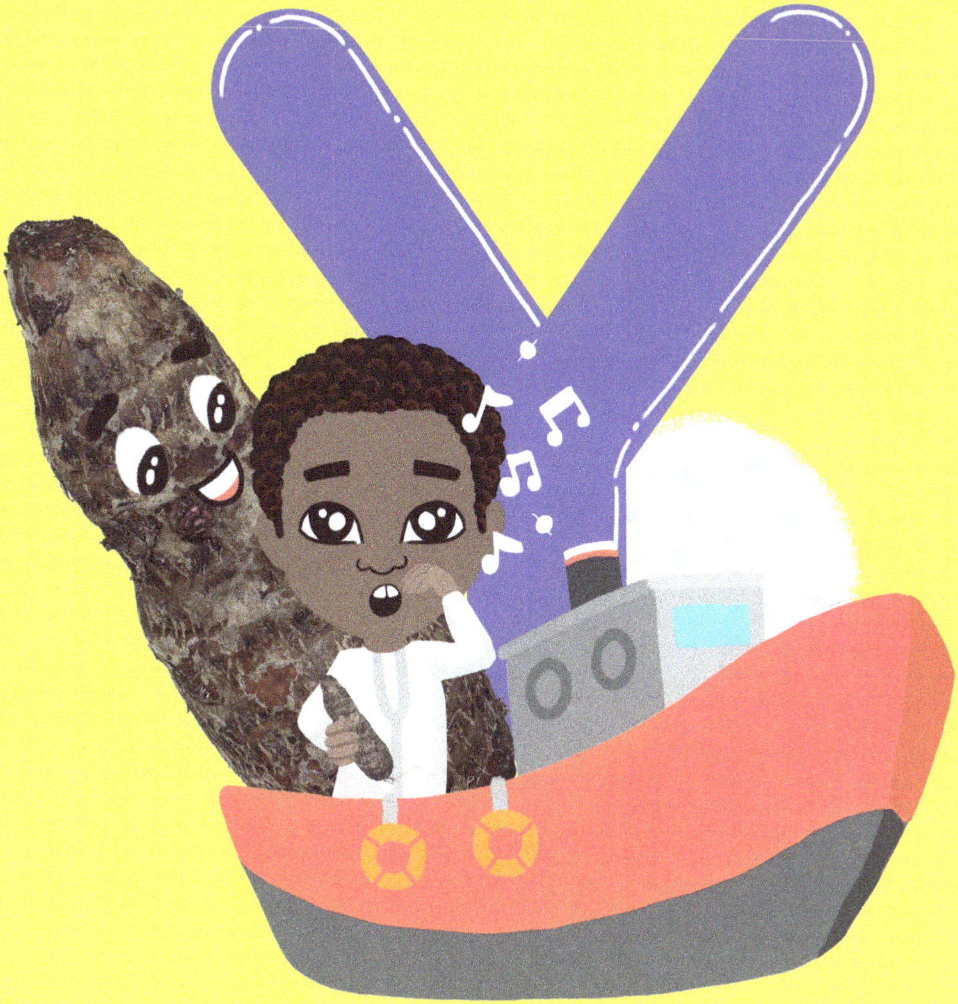

Yy

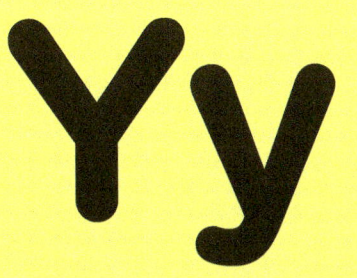

Y IS FOR YAM

Yousef **y**odels for **y**ams
on a **y**acht.

Zz

Z IS FOR ZUCCHINI
Zoey feeds **z**ebras **z**ucchini at the **z**oo.

Aa Bb Cc Dd Ee Ff

Gg Hh Ii Jj Kk Ll

Mm Nn Oo Pp Qq

Rr Ss Tt Uu Vv

Ww Xx Yy Zz

Visit us on the web! www.kidfoodexplorers.com